D0544442

Cricket

SPORTS SKILLS

Chris Oxlade

FRANKLIN WATTS

LONDON•SYDNEY

Franklin Watts
Published in Great Britain in 2017
by The Watts Publishing Group

Credits

Series Editor: Adrian Cole
Art direction: Peter Scoulding
Series designed and created for
 Franklin Watts by Storeybooks
Designer: Rita Storey
Editor: Nicola Barber
Photography: Tudor Photography,
Banbury (unless otherwise stated)
Illustrations: Nigel Kitching

Dewey number 796.3'58
ISBN 978 1 4451 5243 1

Printed in Dubai

MIX
Paper from
responsible sources
FSC www.fsc.org FSC® C104740

Franklin Watts
An imprint of Hachette Children's Group
Part of The Watts Publishing Group
Carmelite House
50 Victoria Embankment
London EC4Y 0DZ

An Hachette UK Company
www.hachette.co.uk

www.franklinwatts.co.uk

Note: At the time of going to press, the
statistics and player profiles in this book were
up to date. However, due to some players'
active participation in the sport, it is possible
that some of these may now be out of date.

Picture credits

Action plus/Neil Tingle p.6; Action plus/
Mike King p.7; Action plus/Adam Bailey
p.8; Corbis/Howard Burditt p.9; Wikimedia
Commons p.9; Action plus/Glyn Kirk p.17;
Getty Images/Gareth Copley p.17; Action
plus/Neil Tingle p.18; Action plus/Glyn Kirk
p.19; Bettmann/Corbis p20; Action plus/Glyn
Kirk p.21; Getty Images/Gareth Copley p.23;
Action plus/Glyn Kirk p25; Action plus/Glyn
Kirk p26.

Cover images: Tudor Photography, Banbury.

All photos posed by models.

Thanks to Hassan Ahmed, Joel Avery,
John Rutland and Joseph White.

The Publisher would like to thank the Banbury
Cricket Club for the use of
their ground.

Previously published by Franklin Watts as
Know Your Sport: Cricket

Taking part in sport is a fun
way to get fit, but like any
form of physical exercise it has
an element of risk, particularly
if you are unfit, overweight
or suffer from any medical
conditions. It is advisable
to consult a healthcare
professional before beginning
any programme of exercise.

Contents

What is Cricket?   6

Cricket Around the World   8

Equipment   10

Overs, Runs and Wickets   12

Bowling   14

Seam and Swing Bowling   16

Spin Bowling   18

Batting   20

Defence and Attack   22

More Attacking Strokes   24

Fielding   26

Statistics and Records   28

Glossary and Websites   29

Index   30

What is Cricket?

Cricket is a bat-and-ball game played between two teams of 11 players. It is a game packed with tension and excitement. Bowlers hurl the ball at immense speed or use cunning spin. Batsmen battle to defend their wickets, play powerful strokes, sprint for runs and smash the ball high over the boundary. Fielders leap to take spectacular catches. And there are many nail-biting finishes.

The Teams

A team contains batsmen, bowlers and a wicket-keeper. Players who are good at both batting and bowling are known as all-rounders. One of the 11 players in the team is the captain.

The Field of Play

Cricket is played on a large grass area. In the middle is a rectangular area called the pitch, where the bowlers bowl and the batsmen bat. At the ends of the pitch, 20 metres apart, are two wooden wickets. In front of each wicket is a white line called the crease. Batsmen run between these lines. The rest of the field of play is called the outfield, and the edge of the outfield is called the boundary.

The picture below shows the positions in the field of play. To see a more detailed diagram of fielding positions see page 26.

Boundary Wicket Umpire Fielder
Wicket-keeper Batsman Wicket
Batsman Umpire
Crease Pitch Bowler

Batting and Bowling

A cricket match is played in 'innings'. During an innings, one team bats and the other fields. At the start of a match, the two captains toss a coin to decide who bats first. Each side has one or two innings in a match. The batting side tries to score as many runs as possible.

Meanwhile, the bowlers on the fielding side bowl the ball at the batsmen to try to get them out and stop them scoring. An innings finishes when ten of the 11 batsmen are out, or the number of overs allowed for the innings is bowled.

Umpires

Every match is controlled by two umpires. The most important task for the umpires is to judge whether a batsman is out or not. An umpire's decision is final. In professional matches there is often a third umpire who watches television replays to help make decisions.

An over is a group of six balls which are known as 'deliveries'. The side that scores the most runs wins the match. Matches can also be tied or drawn.

These boys are playing cricket on a piece of waste ground in Mumbai, India. Cricket can be played almost anywhere as long as you have a ball and a bat.

● It's a Fact

Cricket is believed to have been invented more than 400 years ago in England. The first rules were written down in 1744. The first full international match, or 'Test match' was played between England and Australia in 1877.

7

Cricket Around the World

Cricket is played in many different parts of the world, but is most popular in Australia, England, New Zealand, South Africa, South Asia and the West Indies. It is played in schools, in local leagues, national leagues and internationally. Matches vary in length from a few hours to five whole days.

One-day Cricket

Some cricket matches are played in one day. Each side has one innings, which lasts for a set number of overs, for example 40 or 50 per side. This form of cricket is known

The World Cup

The World Cup is a tournament of one day cricket played every four years. The first World Cup was for women, in 1973, and was won by England. In 1975 the West Indies won the first men's World Cup.

as one-day or limited-overs cricket. 'Twenty20' cricket is an exciting version of the game, with just 20 overs allowed for each side.

England play Pakistan under floodlights at a match in South Africa.

Multi-day Cricket

Matches with two innings per side are played over three, four or five days. These matches are normally played in national championships, such as the County Championship in England and the Sheffield Shield in Australia. International matches are known as Test matches. The men's Test series is made up of several five-day matches played between two of the Test-playing countries: Australia, Bangladesh, England, India, New Zealand, Pakistan, South Africa, Sri Lanka, the West Indies and Zimbabwe.

Kwik Cricket

Kwik Cricket (called MILO in2CRICKET in Australia and ActivePost Kiwi Cricket in New Zealand) is a fun version of cricket for young children

played with plastic balls, bats and stumps. It helps children to learn cricket skills before they move on to playing with a hard ball.

Making the Rules

International cricket is organised by the International Cricket Council (ICC). The Marylebone Cricket Club (MCC), at Lord's Cricket Ground in London, England, is the guardian of the Laws of Cricket, which are the rules of the game. Each country has its own governing body, such as the England and Wales Cricket Board (ECB) and Cricket Australia.

A professional player teaches a group of young cricketers with Kwik Cricket equipment.

The Ashes

The Ashes Test series takes place every two years between England and Australia is played for a small urn called the Ashes. It is said that inside the urn are the ashes of a bail that was burned after Australia beat England in 1882.

Equipment

Playing cricket requires special equipment. Wearing the correct clothing or shoes is not essential, but safety equipment is vital if you are playing with a hard cricket ball as it can cause serious injuries.

The maximum size allowed for a cricket bat is 96.5cm long and 10.8cm across.

Bats

- The main part of a cricket bat, the 'blade', is made out of willow wood. The handle is made from cane, and covered with a rubber grip.
- Bats come in different sizes and weights. Light bats weigh about 1.1kg while heavy bats weigh about 1.3kg. Always use the correct size bat for your height and weight.

The Ball

- A cricket ball is made from layers of cork and string, covered with polished leather. The finished ball weighs about 160g, and measures about 22.6cm round the middle.
- Most cricket balls are red, but white balls are used for day-night games because they are easier to see under floodlights.

• Top Tip

A cricket bat needs to be oiled occasionally with special cricket-bat oil, to stop the wood drying out. A new bat must also be hit all over the flat face and edges with a cricket ball. This is called knocking-in. It helps to stop the surface cracking.

The two halves of leather that cover a cricket ball are stitched together to make a seam around the ball.

Stumps and Bails

- A wicket is made up of three stumps with two wooden bails resting on top.
- The three wooden stumps are each 71cm high and are placed in the ground to make a wicket measuring 23cm across.
- Special heavy bails may be used in windy weather.

Clothing and Protection

Traditional cricket clothing is mainly white, but coloured uniforms are used in many one-day competitions, including day–night games. Clothing is loose-fitting, which allows players to keep cool and move about easily. Cricket shoes have spikes or studs for grip on the grass. Hats and sunblock are important when the sun shines. Cricket gloves, pads and helmets are worn by batsmen, wicket-keepers and some close fielders to provide some protection against being injured by the hard ball.

Batsmen wear pads on their legs, a groin protector, padded gloves and a helmet with a face guard. Sometimes they also wear thigh, chest and arm pads.

The New Ball

During play the shine on a new ball gradually wears away. The leather becomes rough and the ball softens.

A new ball is normally used for each game, and for the start of each innings. But during multi-day matches, the ball can be replaced in the middle of an innings.

Overs, Runs and Wickets

The progress of an innings is measured in overs, runs and wickets. A bowler bowls balls (or deliveries) in groups of six, called overs. At the end of an over, a different bowler bowls from the other end of the pitch.

A page from a cricket scorebook. Batsmen's scores are recorded in the top section and bowlers' overs in the bottom section.

Scoring Runs

One batsman, called the striker, defends the wicket at the opposite end of the pitch to the bowler. The non-striker stands at the bowler's end. When the striker hits the ball into the field the batsmen can run. A run is scored when both batsmen pass each other and reach the batting crease (see page 6) at the opposite end of the pitch. The batsmen can turn and run back again to score a second and even a third and fourth run.

Four runs are automatically scored if the ball reaches the boundary, and six are scored if the ball crosses the boundary before bouncing.

Recording the Score

The score is recorded by scorers in a special scorebook. This has space to record all the details of an innings, such as the runs scored from each ball, when wickets fall, the number of overs bowled, the overall total, and so on. The score is also displayed on a scoreboard for the benefit of players and spectators.

Batsmen crossing in the middle of the pitch as they run.

Extras

Extras are runs that are not scored by the batsmen.

They are awarded for:
- No-balls and wides (see page 15), which are mistakes by a bowler.
- Byes (the striker does not touch the ball and the batsmen run).
- Leg-byes (the ball hits the batsman on the body and the batsmen run).

Umpires

One umpire stands behind the stumps at the bowler's end, and the other stands to the side of the striker. The umpires' most important job is to decide when a batsman is dismissed. Umpires also count the number of balls, decide whether a bowler has bowled a no-ball or a wide, and indicate if a batsman has hit a four or a six.

The Signals

Extras

The umpires give signals to the scorers and players to indicate extras, boundaries and wickets.

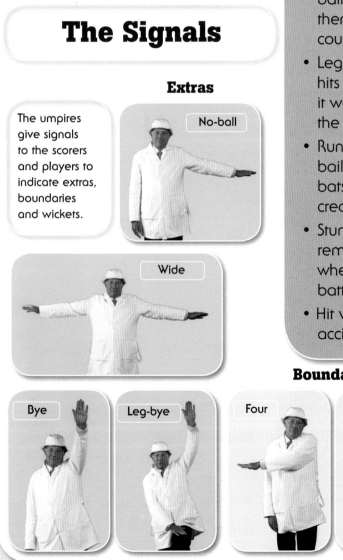

No-ball

Wide

Bye

Leg-bye

Wickets

When a batsman is dismissed (or out), his wicket is 'lost'. The main ways that batsmen lose their wickets are:

- Bowled: the ball hits the wicket, making one or both bails fall off.
- Caught: the batsman hits the ball in the air and it is caught by a fielder before it bounces. If the ball hits the batsman's glove and then is caught by a fielder, it is counted as being out.
- Leg-before-wicket (lbw): the ball hits the batsmen's leg when it would have gone on to hit the stumps.
- Run out: a fielder removes the bails with the ball before a batsman reaches the batting crease.
- Stumped: the wicket-keeper removes the bails with the ball when the batsman is outside his batting crease.
- Hit wicket: the batsman accidentally knocks off the bails.

Boundaries

Four

Six

Wicket

Out

13

Bowling

The aim of bowling is to get the batsmen out or stop them scoring runs. There are two main styles of bowling: seam and swing (see page 16), and spin (see page 18). Seam and swing bowlers bowl much faster than spin bowlers. The fastest bowlers can bowl at 145km/h. Bowlers normally make the ball bounce once before it reaches the batsman.

Accurate Bowling

Bowlers try to bowl a good 'line and length'. Line is the direction of the delivery. Length is how far in front of the batsman the ball bounces. A good-length ball bounces one or two metres in front of the batsman. A short-pitched delivery bounces further away, and an over-pitched delivery bounces closer. Bowling a good line and length makes it hard for batsmen to hit the ball away for runs.

The Bowling Action

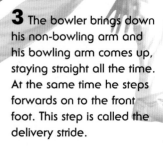

1 The bowler begins with a run-up to build up speed.

2 At the end of the run-up, and just before the ball is delivered, the bowler is side-on to the pitch. The non-bowling arm is raised and the bowler's weight is on the back foot.

3 The bowler brings down his non-bowling arm and his bowling arm comes up, staying straight all the time. At the same time he steps forwards on to the front foot. This step is called the delivery stride.

No-balls and Wides

The bowler's front foot must not go beyond the batting crease at the moment the ball is bowled, otherwise the umpire calls the delivery a no-ball.

A wide is a delivery so far either side of the wicket that, in the opinion of the umpire, the batsman cannot reach it. A no-ball or wide gives an extra run to the batting side, and the ball must be bowled again.

4 The ball is released just as the bowling arm starts to come down again. The bowler follows through so that his arm passes by his knees.

When a bowler thinks the batsman is caught or lbw, he shouts 'How was that?' (normally shortened to 'Howzat?') at the umpire. This is known as making an appeal. The umpire either replies 'Not out', or raises his first finger, the signal that the batsman is out. The appeal is very important. If there is no appeal, the umpire cannot give a batsman out.

Left or Right?

The photographs on these pages show a left-handed bowler. Everything is reversed for right-handed bowlers. Bowlers can decide which side of the wicket to bowl from.

Seam and Swing Bowling

Seam and swing bowlers (or seamers) try to get batsmen out by making the ball move sideways as it travels down the pitch. This is to deceive the batsman into missing the ball or giving a catch. The ball 'seams' if it changes direction when it hits the pitch. 'Swing' is when the ball bends or curves in the air before it bounces.

Grip for Seam and Swing

To bowl seam or swing, a bowler holds the ball with the seam vertical. As the bowler lets go, he flicks his wrist forwards to give the ball extra speed and to make it rotate backwards. The rotation helps keep the seam upright as the ball is in the air.

Seaming In and Away

If the bowler gets his action right, the ball lands on its seam. This can make it move slightly into or away from the batsman.

The faster the ball is bowled, the less time the batsman has to react. The ball tends to seam more if the pitch is damp, grassy or cracked.

Adding Swing

If a bowler holds the ball with the seam at a slight angle, the ball may swing through the air. A swinging ball is either an outswinger or an inswinger.

Some bowlers swing the ball naturally, but others find it very hard to swing the ball at all. The ball normally swings more in humid weather. Bowlers polish one side of the ball to keep it shiny and allow the other side to become dull and rough. The ball swings in the direction of the shiny side.

The grip for basic seam bowling. The seam points straight down the pitch.

Gripping the ball for the outswinger.

Gripping the ball for the inswinger.

Reverse Swing

When a ball has been used for about 40 overs or more it can begin to swing in the opposite direction to normal. This is called reverse swing. Bowlers allow one side of the ball to get scuffed to help to create reverse swing.

Stuart Broad

England
Right-arm fast medium bowler
Date of birth: 24 June, 1986
Test debut: 2007 v Sri Lanka
Test matches: 98
Wickets: 358
Average: 29.90 runs per wicket
Best innings: 8 for 15 (2015 v Australia)

Stuart Broad has the ability to produce great performances when needed. In 2009, his five for 37 against Australia helped England to retain the Ashes.

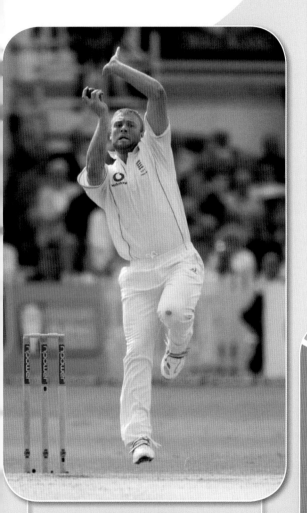

A fast bowler leaps into the air before landing on his back foot for the delivery stride. This photo shows former England international Andrew Flintoff in action.

Surprise Deliveries

A good fast bowler will sometimes try to deceive the batsman with a surprise delivery. A 'bouncer' is a ball that is pitched very short and bounces very high. A 'yorker' is pitched at a batsman's feet to try to bowl him or trap him lbw. Fast bowlers also bowl slower balls to confuse the batsman into playing a shot before the ball arrives.

Spin Bowling

Spin bowlers try to get batsmen out by making the ball spin one way or the other as it bounces on the pitch. This could make the batsman give a catch, miss the ball and be bowled, trapped lbw or stumped. There are two main types of spin bowling: off-spin and leg-spin.

Off-spin

An off-spinner uses his fingers to make the ball spin. The action is similar to turning a door knob. A right-handed off-spinner spins the ball clockwise as he releases it. This makes the ball turn to the right when it bounces. A left-arm spinner is left-handed, and turns the ball the opposite way.

Leg-spin

A leg-spinner uses a flick of the wrist to make the ball turn. A right-handed leg-spinner spins the ball anti-clockwise as he releases it. This makes the ball turn to the left when it bounces. A left-handed leg-spinner turns the ball the opposite way.

Shane Warne

Australia
Leg-spin bowler
Date of birth: 13 September, 1969
Test debut: 1992 v India
Test matches: 145
Wickets: 708
Average: 25.15 runs per wicket
Best innings: 8 for 71 (1994 v England)

Shane Warne is a legendary Australian leg-spin bowler who retired from cricket in 2007. He was capable of bowling an incredible variety of deliveries to keep batsmen guessing. He took over 1,000 international wickets in his career.

How a bowler grips the ball for leg-spin.

How a bowler grips the ball for off-spin.

Spinners' Tactics

By bowling a good line and length, spin bowlers make it hard for batsmen to score runs. Fielders often stand near to the batsman in the hope of taking a catch. Leg-spinners often bowl into rough footmarks left by bowlers at the other end of the pitch, which can make the ball turn sharply. Spinners also use 'flight' to fool batsmen. This means that the ball is hard to follow in the air, and does not land where the batsman expects.

Spinners' Tricks

Spinners may bowl deliveries that do not spin as the batsman is anticipating. An off-spinner can bowl a delivery that does not turn, or that swings a little the other way. Good leg-spinners have a range of surprise deliveries, such as the 'googly'. A googly turns the opposite way to a normal leg-spin delivery. Leg-spinners can also bowl top-spinners that spin forwards, usually with a lower and faster bounce.

Muttiah Muralitharan

Sri Lanka
Off-spin bowler
Date of birth: 17 April, 1972
Test debut: 1992 v Australia
Test matches: 133
Wickets: 800
Average: 22.72 runs per wicket
Best innings: 9 for 51 (2002 v Zimbabwe)

Muttiah Muralitharan ('Murali') is the most successful Test match bowler of all time. His flexible wrist allows him to spin the ball more than other off-spinners. Muralitharan bowls with a slightly bent arm and is the first player to take 800 Test wickets.

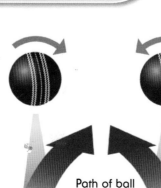

The batsman sees the ball spinning clockwise.

The batsman sees the ball spinning anti-clockwise.

How the ball turns for leg-spin and off-spin seen from the batsman's end of the pitch.

Leg-spin

Path of ball after bouncing

Off-spin

Batting

A batsman's job is to score runs for his team and at the same time to defend his wicket. In a one-day match, batsmen try to score runs as quickly as possible. In a multi-day game batsmen take fewer risks as they try to build a large total.

Batting Order

The first two batsmen to bat are called the openers. They are followed by more top-order batsmen. Then come the middle-order batsmen, who normally include the wicket-keeper and the all-rounders. Last to bat are the bowlers. Often, they are not good batsmen, and are known as tail-enders.

Donald Bradman

Australia
Top-order batsman
Date of birth: 27 August, 1908
Test debut: 1928 v England
Test matches: 52
Runs scored: 6996
Batting average: 99.94 runs
Highest score: 334 (1930 v England)

Sir Donald Bradman ('The Don') was the greatest batsman of all. His success came from incredible concentration. Unfortunately, he was out for no runs in his last Test innings, when he needed just four runs for a Test average of 100.

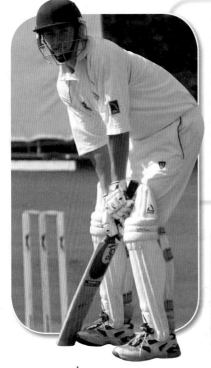

The stance for a right-handed batsman. The end of the bat rests on the ground and his hands rest on the front pad.

The batting grip for a right-handed batsman. The hands are reversed for a left-handed batsman.

The Stance

It is important for a batsman to stand in the correct position to defend his stumps. This is known as taking up a stance. He should stand relaxed with his feet slightly apart and the bat resting on the ground.

The batsman stands on the batting crease, with his feet just outside the line of the leg stump. A batsman always 'takes guard' before facing his first ball. He makes a mark on the pitch in line with one of the stumps so that he knows exactly where to stand without having to look back at the stumps.

Calling for Runs

When the striker hits the ball, he and the non-striker must decide whether to run. The batsman who can see the ball and fielders more easily makes calls to the other batsman. 'Yes' means take a run. 'No' means do not run. 'Wait' means get ready but do not run yet.

Brian Lara

West Indies
Top-order batsman
Date of birth: 2 May, 1969
Test debut: 1990 v Pakistan
Test matches: 131
Runs scored: 11,953
Batting average: 52.88 runs
Highest score: 400 not out (2004 v England)

A left-handed batsman, Brian Lara holds the records for both the highest individual Test score (400 not out) and the highest first-class score (501 not out). He was also captain of the West Indies team.

As the bowler bowls, the batsman raises his bat and gets into position for the shot.

A batsman is safe if he 'grounds' his bat inside the crease at the end of a run.

Defence and Attack

As soon as the bowler releases the ball, the batsman must quickly work out the length and line of the delivery. He can then decide whether to play a defensive stroke or an attacking shot.

The Forward Defensive

This stroke is played to a ball that is on a good length and is directed at the wicket. It is hard to score off this sort of ball, so the batsman simply tries to stop it hitting the wicket. He steps forwards and brings the bat alongside the front pad. The bat comes down on the ball, hitting it into the ground, and giving no chance of a catch.

The Backward Defensive

This stroke is played to a ball that is short of a good length but could hit the top of the stumps. If the batsman played a forward defensive stroke, the ball could hit his gloves and bounce off to be caught. Instead, he steps back and brings the bat down to meet the ball at waist height, again hitting the ball downwards to avoid being

The Forward Defensive

1 The batsman stands very still, watching the bowler approaching the wicket.

2 The batsman sees that the ball is a good-length, straight ball. He steps forwards towards where the ball is going to bounce (the 'pitch of the ball').

3 He brings the bat down close to his pad, forming a wide barrier. He keeps the bat angled towards the ground. His head is over the bat.

caught. He can hit the ball either towards the 'off side' or the 'leg side'. The off side is the side his chest points to. The leg side is the side behind his legs.

Driving

If the ball is pitched up and not too wide, the batsman can play an attacking stroke called the front-foot drive. He steps forwards to where the ball is going to bounce and swings the bat through powerfully. The drive can be played through the off side, straight along the pitch or through the leg side. It can also be played off the batsman's back foot.

Charlotte Edwards

England
Top-order cricketer
Date of birth: 17 December, 1979
Test debut: 1996 v New Zealand
Test matches: 23
Runs scored: 1676
Batting average: 44.10 runs
Highest score: 173 not out (World Cup 1997 v Ireland)

Charlotte Edwards made her debut playing for England against New Zealand at the age of 16. In 2013 she captained the England team to back-to-back Ashes wins.

The Backward Defensive

1 The batsman sees that the ball is straight and short-pitched. He steps backwards.

2 The batsman stands tall and brings his bat down straight with his left elbow held high.

Leaving the Ball

Batsmen sometimes let balls go past them without trying to hit them. They normally leave a ball that is wide outside the off stump. If they tried to hit the ball they would risk being caught.

More Attacking Strokes

Defensive strokes and attacking drives are played by keeping the bat vertical as it swings through. This is known as playing with a straight bat. Other attacking strokes, such as pulls and cuts, are played with the bat horizontal. This is known as a cross-batted stroke.

The Pull and the Hook

A batsman plays the pull stroke to a ball that is pitched very short and arrives at the batsman at a height between his waist and shoulder. The batsman normally hits the ball downwards along the ground, but can deliberately hit it high into the air to try to get a six. The hook is similar to the pull, but is played to a short-pitched ball that bounces above shoulder height. The batsman swings the bat across in front of his face.

The Sweep

The sweep is a stroke played against a spinner to a good-length ball that is aimed towards leg stump. The batsman goes down on one knee and hits the ball as

Playing the Pull or Hook

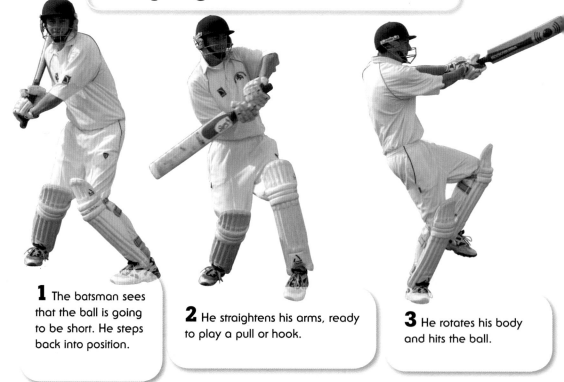

1 The batsman sees that the ball is going to be short. He steps back into position.

2 He straightens his arms, ready to play a pull or hook.

3 He rotates his body and hits the ball.

it bounces, sweeping it round the corner towards the leg side. The 'paddle' is a very gentle sweep. The 'slog' sweep is a full-blooded stroke aimed at scoring a boundary.

The Leg Glance

The leg glance is played to a delivery aimed at the batsman's legs or rest of his body. The batsman holds the bat vertically with the face of the bat angled towards the leg side. The ball glances off the face of the bat.

The Cut

The cut is a cross-batted stroke played through the off side. It is played on the back foot to a short-pitched ball outside off stump. The late cut is a delicate shot played into the field behind the wicket.

Jacques Kallis

South Africa
Top-order batsman
Date of birth: 16 October, 1975
Test debut: 1995 v England
Test matches: 166
Runs scored: 13,289
Batting average: 55.37 runs
Highest score: 224
Bowling average: 32.65 runs per wicket

Jacques Kallis has been described by some as 'the greatest cricketer to play the game' and is acknowledged to be one of the game's finest all-rounders.

Playing the Cut

1 The batsman sees that the ball is short and wide. He steps back and across.

2 The batsman swipes the ball powerfully away.

3 The face of the bat is angled downwards to hit the ball low, avoiding a catch.

Fielding

When a team is fielding, one player, the wicket-keeper, stands behind the wicket at the striker's end. One player is always needed to bowl, leaving nine remaining players who are fielders. The main skills needed by fielders are gathering the ball when it is hit by the batsman, throwing and catching.

Field Placements

The bowler and captain decide where to put their fielders. Some stand close to the pitch to try to take catches. Some are placed to stop the batsman taking single runs and some are placed deep in the outfield to stop boundaries.

Wicket-keeping

The wicket-keeper's job is to catch balls that a batsman leaves or misses, and receive throws from the fielders. The wicket-keeper is the most important fielder. He takes more catches than other fielders and can also stump batsmen if they are outside the batting crease. The wicket-keeper stands close behind the stumps for spin bowlers and further back for fast bowlers.

Gathering and Throwing

Fielders must be alert and ready when the ball is bowled. If the ball is hit straight at them, fielders try to get down low and use both hands to gather the ball. If the ball

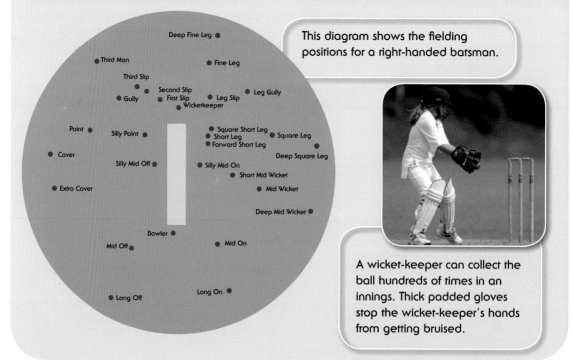

This diagram shows the fielding positions for a right-handed batsman.

Deep Fine Leg
Third Man
Fine Leg
Third Slip
Second Slip
Leg Gully
Gully
First Slip
Leg Slip
Wicketkeeper
Point
Silly Point
Square Short Leg
Short Leg
Square Leg
Forward Short Leg
Cover
Deep Square Leg
Silly Mid Off
Silly Mid On
Short Mid Wicket
Extra Cover
Mid Wicket
Deep Mid Wicket
Bowler
Mid Off
Mid On
Long On
Long Off

A wicket-keeper can collect the ball hundreds of times in an innings. Thick padded gloves stop the wicket-keeper's hands from getting bruised.

is about to run over the boundary, the fielder slides along the ground and flicks the ball back to save a boundary being scored. As soon as a fielder has gathered the ball he throws it back to the wicket-keeper as quickly and accurately as possible. Good fielders can run out a batsman with a direct hit on the stumps if the batsman is outside the batting crease.

Catching

Taking catches is very important. A dropped catch can cost the fielding side a lot of runs if the batsman goes on to get a high score.

Overthrows and Backing Up

An inaccurate throw from a fielder can miss the wicket-keeper and run into the outfield. This allows the batsmen to run again. These extra runs are called overthrows. A fielder normally stands behind the wicket-keeper when the throw is coming in to prevent overthrows. This is called backing up.

Catches can come low and fast or from high in the air. Some players are specialist slip or gully catchers (see diagram on page 26).

A high catch is taken with the fingers pointed upwards.

Close catchers, such as this slip fielder, crouch down before the ball is bowled, ready to receive a catch.

Getting down ready to stop the ball. This position is called the long barrier. If the fielder lets the ball go through his hands, his leg provides an extra 'long barrier' to stop the ball.

Statistics and Records

Highest Team Test Scores

952 for 6	Sri Lanka	1997 v India
903 for 7	England	1938 v Australia
849 all out	England	1930 v West Indies
790 for 3	West Indies	1958 v Pakistan
765 for 6	Pakistan	2009 v Sri Lanka

Most Test Wickets

800	Muttiah Muralitharan	Sri Lanka
708	Shane Warne	Australia
619	Anil Kumble	India
563	Glenn McGrath	Australia
519	Courtney Walsh	West Indies

Highest Individual Test Scores

400 not out	Brian Lara	West Indies	2004 v England
380	Matthew Hayden	Australia	2003 v Zimbabwe
375	Brian Lara	West Indies	1994 v England
374	Mahela Jayawardene	Sri Lanka	2006 v South Africa
365 not out	Garry Sobers	West Indies	1958 v Pakistan

Lowest Team Test Score

26 all out   New Zealand   1955 v England

Most Test Runs

15,921   Sachin Tendulkar   India

Six Sixes

The first batsman to hit six sixes in one over was Garry Sobers, in a county match in Swansea, Wales in 1968.

All Ten Wickets in a Test Innings

10 for 53	Jim Laker	England	1956 v Australia
10 for 74	Anil Kumble	India	1999 v Pakistan

Most Test Centuries

51   Sachin Tendulkar   India

Most One-day Wickets

534   Muttiah Muralitharan   Sri Lanka

Highest One-day Team Score

444 for 3   England   2016 v Pakistan

Highest One-day Individual Score

264   Rohit Sharma   India 2014 v Sri Lanka

Fastest Bowler

The fastest delivery was bowled in 2003 by Shoaib Akhtar of Pakistan. Its speed was electronically measured at 161.3km/h.

Most Wicket-keeping Test Wickets

555 (532 catches; 23 stumpings)   Mark Boucher   S Africa

Fastest One-day Century

31 balls   AB de Villiers   South Africa   2015 v W Indies

Glossary

All-rounder A player who is both a good batsman and a good bowler.

Bails The pieces of wood that sit on top of the stumps.

Batting crease The line drawn across the pitch in front of the wicket.

Boundary 1) The edge of a cricket field; 2) When the ball is hit to the boundary.

Bowled When a delivery hits the wicket.

Close fielder A fielder who stands near to the batsman.

Covers The area square of the pitch on the off side.

Day–night game A match that starts in the afternoon and continues into the evening.

Delivery When a bowler bowls the ball.

Lbw A batsman is lbw if the umpire believes that the ball would have hit the stumps had it not been obstructed by the batsman's pads.

Leg side The side behind a batsman's legs.

Leg-spin Spin bowling that makes the ball spin in from outside the leg.

Length How far in front of a batsman a delivery lands.

Line The line of a delivery along the pitch.

No ball An illegal delivery by a bowler

Off side The side a batsman's chest faces.

Off-spin Spin bowling that makes the ball spin in from outside the off stump of a right-handed batsman.

Over Six deliveries by a bowler

Pitch A rectangular area that is mowed and rolled.

Run out When a fielder hits the wicket with the ball before the batsman reaches the crease.

Seam bowling Bowling that uses the seam on the ball to make the ball change direction.

Slips The area close behind a batsman slightly on the off side.

Stumps Vertical wooden posts. A wicket has three stumps.

Swing bowling Bowling that makes the ball swing through the air.

Wicket 1) The target that bowlers aim at; 2) when a batsman is dismissed.

Wicket-keeper The fielder who stands behind the wicket.

Wide A delivery too wide for a batsman to reach.

Index

appeals 15
Ashes 9, 17, 23
attack 22–3, 24–5

backing up 27
backward defensive 22–3
bails 11, 13
balls 10
bats 10
batsmen 6, 12–20, 23, 26
batting 7, 20–1, 22–3, 24–5
batting order 20
bouncers 17
boundaries (scoring) 12, 13, 25, 26
boundary 6, 7, 12, 27
bowled (out) 13
bowlers 6, 12, 14–20
bowling 7, 14–15, 16–17, 18–19
Bradman, Donald 20
Broad, Stuart 17
byes 12, 13

catching 26, 27
caught (out) 13
clothing 11
crease 6, 12, 13, 15, 21, 26
cross-batted strokes 24–5
cuts 24, 25

day–night games 11
defence 20, 22–3, 24
deliveries 7, 12, 14–15
driving 23

Edwards, Charlotte 23
extras 12

fast bowlers 17

field of play 6
fielding 6, 26–7
flight 19
Flintoff, Andrew 17
forward defensive 22

gathering 26–7
googly 19
grounding the bat 21

history of cricket 7
hit wicket 13
hooks 24
Howzat? 15

innings 7, 8, 9, 11, 12
inswingers 16

Kallis, Jacques 25
Kwik Cricket 9

Lara, Brian 21
lbw (leg-before-wicket) 13, 15, 17, 18
left-handers 15, 18
leg-byes 12, 13
leg glances 25
leg-spin 18, 19
line and length 14–15

multi-day cricket 9, 20
Muralitharan, Muttiah 19

no-balls 12, 13, 15

off-spin 18, 19
one-day cricket 8, 11, 20
outfield 7
outswingers 16
overs 7, 8, 12, 17
overthrows 27

pads 11

pitch 6, 12, 16, 20, 21, 26
pulls 24

rules 9
run out 13
run-up 14
runs 6, 7, 12, 14, 15, 19, 20, 21, 26, 27

safety equipment 10, 11
scoring 12
seam bowling 14, 16
signals 13
spin bowling 18–19
stance 21
straight bat 24
stumped 13, 18
stumps 9, 11, 13, 21, 22, 23, 24, 25, 26, 27
sweeps 25
swing bowling 14, 16–17

taking guard 21
teams 6, 7, 20, 26
Test matches 7, 9, 19, 20, 21
throwing 26, 27
Twenty20 cricket 8

umpires 6, 7, 13, 15

Warne, Shane 18
wicket-keepers 6, 11, 13, 20, 26, 27
wickets 6, 11, 12, 13, 15, 18, 19, 20, 22, 25
wides 12, 13, 15
World Cup 8

yorkers 17